GENERIC THOUGHTS

EXPLORATIONS IN THE REALM OF RANDOMNESS

ZAID ASGHAR

Made with ♥ on the Notion Press Platform
www.notionpress.com

To the one I love, nurture and protect.

To my Rose.

Contents

Contents

Contents

Contents

Contents

FOREWORD

The quest for your immortality ends with revelation
- Stranger

Preface

I offer a collection of diverse experiences and reflections
on emotions and existence. What sets this book apart is its
foundation in real-life situations, emotions, and personal
encounters. Some sections are inspired by careful
observation and analysis, while others stem from firsthand
experiences that prompted deep contemplation.
Encountering similar situations, I felt compelled to share
insights with loved ones on navigating life's challenges.
The remaining content delves into my perspective on
various aspects of existence and the emotions evoked by
specific encounters. The primary aim of this book is to
impart insights into human nature that may prove
beneficial to readers

Acknowledgements

I would like to express my heartfelt gratitude to all those
who have supported me throughout this journey. To my
family and friends, your unwavering encouragement and
love have been my greatest source of strength.
I am also grateful to the readers who have embraced
my work and found inspiration within its pages. Your
feedback and support mean the world to me. I would like
to thank someone very special to me, without whom I
wouldn't have the courage to pursue any of my dreams, the
one who broke the barriers of delusions to become reality.
Thank you all for being a part of this wonderful
adventure.

I hope no one looks at you the way I do,
For if they did,
They would fight me to death
Over being near you,
Blessed
By your companionship,
Your warmth,
Your feel.

II

My heart aches for those
Whose hearts have grown cold,
Whose souls strive to smile,
Who secretly long for warmth,
But deem themselves disdained of it.

III

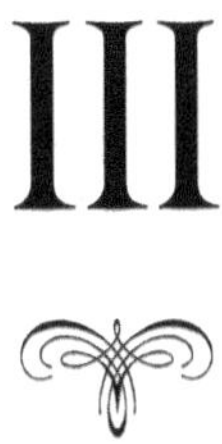

I love how much time it takes to believe.

IV

You see yourself grow,
You see yourself heal,
From the hell you went through.
The patience in you enhances
Your ability to endure,
And let happiness intertwine with you.

Your presence, your presence!
You walk in unexpectedly,
Unintentionally glistening my dull skin,
Making my eyes shine,
Putting my chaotic heart at rest.
Your presence is where I achieve my Nirvana.

VI

I don't get it when you cage yourself,
To the words of the stone-hearted.
There is far to go by than mere words,
You deserve the world and more.
Your happiness should not be subjected,
To thoughts and questions.
Free yourself from this cage,
Experience your true freedom.

VII

We are in a constant battle with ourselves,
About progressing onto good,
Staying content where you are now,
Or to go back and drown in the lake of memories.
Be wise in choosing to focus,
Then be folly and live in distress.

VIII

The depths of the darkness you go through,
And still smile with positivity.
No wonder you are
So compelled, yet so brave.

IX

You remind me of summer after school:
Coming in after a long wait,
Freeing up the trapped souls,
Letting loose the innocence,
A time where most happy memories are made—
The most awaited, the most precious, the most
cherished.

X

Ever pondered the allure of expanding your social horizon? Imagine the dance of time: how it slips away unnoticed amidst the crowd. What if, instead of chasing fleeting connections, you embraced the symphony of self-discovery?

Within the tapestry of faces lies a tale untold—for among the throng, whispers the shadow of deceit. They approach with honeyed words, only to vanish when the melody fades, leaving you stranded in the silence of their absence. Perhaps solitude isn't a curse, but a sanctuary, guarding against the siren's call of false companionship.

XI

Some masks of obnoxiousness are safe.
When you have pushed all the love you got,
Gave up during the fight, leaving people obscure as to
why you never fought back.
The more composed you are with different aspects of
life, the stronger you are.
Everyone has their gifts and their fair share of strengths

XII

Strength knows no bound.
Your strength isn't subjected to only your physicality.
Your uniqueness is your strength.
Your will is your strength.
Your courage is your strength.
Your love is your strength.

XIII

I feel you as the gentle breeze that kicks in at the right
moment.
The shade under which the monsoons are easy.
The light which befalls right over.
You are quite amusing.

XIV

In the fabric of our existence, we often find ourselves entangled in threads of distress, grappling with unanswerable questions that echo through the corridors of our minds. And even when answers grace us with their presence, we shy away from embracing their light, shackled by the weight of unmet expectations. Indeed, life's journey can be an exhausting pilgrimage. From the very moment consciousness dawns upon us, we are confronted with unclaimed sorrows, compelled to erect barriers and retreat into the sanctuary of solitude.

XV

The distance was just a number,
As we began our love's tale to uncover.
A building in progress, we thought we'd be,
But insecurities shook us, you see.
Trust, the cornerstone, crumbled away,
Tremors of doubt, where hearts lay.
Our love, once strong, now torn apart,
By earthquakes of fear, that shattered our heart.

XVI

Don't play fast and loose at life,
Figure out where you are,
And work towards where you would want to be,
Before what you were drags you back,
To where you came from.

XVII

Why do you still need more time?
Clueless how to explain,
Most certain that no one even tried wondering,
And never would they understand how love was,
And is still sublime.

XVIII

Good-byes are never easy; ours was no different.
It was never easy to say the final goodbyes.
I long to walk away from you,
But I find myself hopelessly lost
In memory lane.

XIX

Before we ask questions, we should first look at our comfort zone to just be sure of what we'd want and what we'd be comfortable with.
Honestly speaking, most of our problems would stop with a simple 'no'.

XX

She is,

A matter of pride and happiness. She has her own identity that she embraces every day. She doesn't need to always be referred to as someone's mother, sister, wife, friend, girlfriend.

Why should she be referred to as someone's when she is her own identity? She doesn't need the association with anyone's masculine kin to be respected or acknowledged.

She, just like all living things, is unique. Has her very own identity. She should never be associated with anyone to get respect or love; she should always be embraced for her own originality. She was profound, and she is!

XXI

She was word for word as they described her:
Blossom in her smile,
Fatal by her looks,
Destructive at eyes.
No doubt she's a serene catastrophe.

All your desires are not justified!
As humans, we are an amalgamation of good and bad.
We adapt to what we feel is right, but it doesn't necessarily
mean that it's correct.
All our desires emulate what we are made of: good and
bad. We either learn to control the urge or give in and live a
life of justifying the wrong.

Time again proves that you are for yourself in toughest times, Yet we strive to impress our peers by forcing ourselves into something we're not comfortable with. The urges of human companionship are indeed fascinating; it makes you someone you're not.

XXIV

You are often found forcing yourself to acceptance.
Peer pressure is a malicious form of social intervention;
it urges you to do things you're not comfortable with, but
still, you do it anyway so that you get to blame anyone else
but yourself.

XXV

We abandon what we know,
Follow the trail of what we feel,
In the realms of love where we strive to find each other,
To embrace the oneness of our union, our unity.

XXVI

It took more time than what I had to give you a place in
life.
But it took one moment to say, "Fuck it" and "Fuck you."
Maybe I wasn't really up for you.
Because nothing ceases to exist overnight.

XXVII

In a world where everyone demands to be someone's
queens and kings, try to become their friend.
The kingdoms fall, and empires crumble, but true
friendship lasts a lifetime and beyond.

XXVIII

If only you knew how to put an end to all your melancholy
and pain.
If only life came with a manual.
If only you were taught how to face things the right
way.
If only you never would've done mistakes.
You would never have learnt anything.

XXIX

I know not bliss,
If not her.
Know not serenity,
Know what's real,
If not her.
Know what's true,
Know not love,
If not her.

XXX

Most people crying about toxicity may be highly toxic themselves. In their quest for manifesting goodness and living with positivity, they develop the habit to blame others at their convenience. It's easier to blame than confront their own demons. They're just too ignorant to see what they are until they are left with nothing but a mirror.

XXXI

Your intentions determine your value as a person. Wanting
to be taken as a good person with a deceitful heart is as
though mourning the ones you've murdered. Yes, things
can be fixed. But nothing can be fixed without the correct
intentions. Justifying everything bad that happened to you
without acknowledgment of your faults will lead you
nowhere in your life or others.

XXXII

The originality that we possess should be conserved and preserved.
Whilst we're proud of unruly gestures of ourselves, we should be proud of what we are and who we're made of.

XXXIII

You took whatever I gave you,
And crushed it right in front of me.
And you used that to build what you are now,
And delete me everywhere from your social life,
To your memories.
I now realize the difference between love and
infatuation,
Because I was your moment, and you were my forever.

XXXIV

Mononymous with dejection all the time, I am this now.
For I am haunted by your love, by your hate, pushed by
your awfully malign lies.
To escape your memories, I walk till my feet bleed,
Always with the lowest gaze, I am a man, yet some part
cries,
When I'm reminded of your braids.

XXXV

There are grievances that I have from life. It was never my choice to experience what I did, feel what I felt, deal with things foolishly, being naïve and optimistic. Things life threw at me were never really anticipated, nor thought over. It was any and everything.

You never imagine what someone truly becomes to you when you start to talk; what they might become to you one day is a conundrum. You would feel you are being delusional, but your dejected fate, sometime somewhere, meets optimization in the form of a human. Somethings, if not most, are by design. You can't control meeting them. You can't control not talking to them. You can't help but find solace and tranquility in them.

It's funny how some strangers become your home. Some accidents are your destination.

XXXVII

Now, whatever is right
Or whatever may be wrong,
I'll love you eternally,
In your arms, that I belong.
Meet me in the gardens of love,
Forever I'll hold your hand; I will follow you
everywhere,
Though condescending I am.

All your anger, all your pain, all your sorrows, and all your anguish would be standing in front of you, and you will walk right past them because of the darkness. Maybe it's good sometimes that you're in a dark place.

XXXIX

Frivolous, I am, to hold onto hope,
Marching towards the darkness, walking away from
light.
Questioning reality as I perceive it:
It may give me my haven or destruction.

XL

You never imagine what someone truly becomes to you when you start to talk. What they might become to you one day is a conundrum. You would feel you are being delusional, but your dejected fate, sometime somewhere, meets optimization in the form of a human. Some things, if not most, are by design. You can't control meeting them. You can't control not talking to them. You can't help but find solace and tranquillity in them.

XLI

How fortuitous can love be? It always exists in places we overlook.

XLII

We had arguments; she'd be specious every time,
As we reached our end, parting ways in our prime.
She looked me in my eyes, declared nothing was left,
No feelings, affection, emotions, all bereft.
My heart skipped a beat, in that fleeting moment's
stare,
Believed her words, yet her eyes held a glare.
Contradictions within her, I couldn't deny,
Her words spoke farewell, but her eyes said goodbye.

XLIII

Fulfilled my desire to destroy,
I started to love what I lost.
I'm numb from every possible way,
Even my summer has some odd frost.
I'm longing now and forever,
For just an abbreviation in your books,
I shall never ask anything else,
Even my happiness that you took.

XLIV

The one problem these days is that letting go may be the
worst possible thing.
The fear that strikes the heart is what will happen to
you if you actually went through with it.
But, self-sufficiency is not a myth; you can function on
yourself too. And maybe when you have come to terms
with yourself, you will freely love the person who has put
you in such a state.
Prioritize yourself while you can and figure out your
equation before it's too late.

XLV

I can't sleep.
Thinking of how our time was.
Thinking of your smile,
Your braids.
There are some people
you're stuck with, forever.

XLVI

With you being so in need of the presence of someone to
function daily,
With you being monotonous about venting to someone,
and that you'd never find someone ever again to share and
connect on such said levels,
Trust me, you shall find your someone someday.

XLVII

Sometimes hiding your pain
takes out more than just your smile,
takes out more than your sanity,
takes out more than a part of your soul.

XLVIII

The ghosts of my past
bring sweets of sorrow, shattering my present,
again making me hollow.
I gather my strength, swallow my fears.
I just hope all my today's
make a better tomorrow.

XLIX

The eyes,
Oh, those eyes!
Where the calm oceans are found,
Where the storms run their course,
Where the universe resides.
Most importantly,
What tranquillity!

L

My perception differs, they say, but never accept their mistakes. It is not my perception, but their livelihood, is what I've been debating.

LI

It takes more to trust,
It takes just one to lose it.
One instance,
One such circumstance,
One such lie.

LII

Learn not to frown only, at least once in a while.
Smile with whatever you have left, own your narrative,
live your time.

LIII

Listen closely to every word when we are together,
When nothing is blur.
Listen closely whenever you rest your head on my chest,
Listen to the heart, what it says.
Every heartbeat is a new quest.

LIV

I travel far and wide to urge myself to run away.
My foregone fate is such that I may be in someone's
debt.
I tried everything to forget you.

LV

Every random thought, every random circumstance, and random ideology, and so on. But the thought process of now never allows me to criticize the uncertainty of life now. In a way, I have grown fond of uncertainty, grown fond of the suspense, and my curiosity and intrigue are elevated.

LVI

Set sail to find
The long-lost energy,
The long-lost empathy,
The lost chivalry,
The lost you,
Before it's late.

LVII

The connection, my love,
Is sublime because catastrophe averts
When my eyes meet yours.
All my traumas are kept at bay,
And I'm down on all fours.

LVIII

Live as though I am a slave
To the monstrous numbness I have.
I'm done trying to cover things up,
Getting rid of all my masks.
Maybe someday,
I would Tie up loose ends with myself.

LIX

I am made of melancholy, a fugitive of my past.
I am ruptured emotions I possess, hideous to the world.
Glistening my dull skin is your sublime smile;
With you, my felicity blooms,
To feel your presence, I strive.

LX

Stars align,
Things set in motion.
Your plans work,
Your efforts give results.
Your actions will bear fruit.
Give it time.

LXI

Spent all night talking.
The morning brought you closer.
Barely kept my eyes open,
But loved your head on my shoulder.
I long to share every morning I have with you.

LXII

The more you despise your experience, the more foolish you are. You have experienced and learned from your mistakes, and a sign of wisdom is to do better and try not to repeat them. Be glad life made you who you are today.

LXIII

Never procrastinate on life. Some things need to be addressed, need to be dealt with. Some wants need to be met, some needs need to be fulfilled, on priority.

LXIV

It isn't hard to convince someone you love them if you know what they want to hear.

Sit and think, how much of yourself you've lost and how much of yourself is left for you to carry on. If the insecurity in you dies that you might die alone, that will become your vantage point. Irrelevant of the person in front.

LXVI

In her lies the essence of life's mysteries, a tapestry woven
with qualities both familiar and enigmatic. She defies
categorization, embodying the essence of every living
thing, yet bearing the unmistakable imprint of humanity.
Born with an innate sense of duty, she stands as a beacon
of responsibility amidst uncertainty.
Let us honor her with the love and respect she deserves,
regardless of societal roles or expectations, for within her
lies the potential to illuminate our world in ways yet
unseen.

LXVII

Across the seven seas, a heart beats in tune,
In distant lands, under the same moon's swoon.
Thoughts of meeting, uncertain and frail,
Yet hope persists, like a persistent gale.
Each night, he gazes at the moon's soft glow,
Calculating the distance, in whispers low.
Cherishing the beauty, untouched and pure,
Dreams of the day they'll meet, of that he's sure.

LXVIII

Every ounce of guilt that I have, in every pound of my
flesh,
Has broken my conscience into several bits,
And taken me to the land of my regress.
The grounds of my heart were besieged
By the damsel in distress;
It was abandoned by her a long time ago,
But is still fresh in my memory.

LXIX

Had the fortuitous nature been non-existent, there
would've been nothing that I would've thought myself.
Learning is one of the constants that never gets old. Cheers
to every instance, every memory, every heartbreak, and
every moment.

LXX

Sink,
Drown in my eyes.
Eyes, my pain.
Feed on my lust.
Break these barriers of my delusions,
And become mine.

LXXI

The skies cry with me
When I reminisce the time
Where all I knew was happiness
Where joy knew no bounds
Where I despised the sorrows of life.

LXXII

You will break the shackles, burn the iron of the cages that hold you, and you will start to walk. You will walk far away from all the negativity that holds you back. You will walk a long distance till your feet bleed, and you will fall into a pit. A pit so dark that nothing would be visible. And yet, you continue to walk in search of daylight.

LXXIII

My coffee is black,
And so is my soul.
The only color in my life
Is the color of my rose.

Bursting out with laughter,
While hiding your pain.
You are beyond description;
You put the word 'beauty' to shame.

LXXV

Whenever all your happiness is in a spectrum, and to
end yourself you look at the clock,
Learn to smile through the pain;
Only from the ashes you shall rise again.

LXXVI

Brighter than the sun,
An extremely contagious smile,
Makes my heart pound,
And makes me imagine,
The two of us walking,
Down the aisle.

LXXVII

Some decisions are frivolous,
But are fruitful.
No matter what happens,
Outcome comes in your favour or not,
It would still be the greater good.

LXXVIII

Take me to the roads that wouldn't lead me to
My abomination.
Lead me to believe in you.

LXXIX

How do I define
My battles of everyday with the society and myself?
I tend to ignore a few words, but some get to me
eventually.
I guess humans are bound to succumb
To opinions of the world.

LXXX

To find the eternal light, you must overcome the fear of burning out, the fear of the dark, and the fear of losing. It may help you gain a new perspective on things, which would later help you understand yourself and others around.

LXXXI

The braids, like a shining river,
The beauty of your hair,
The way you lock eyes,
And time stands still,
The wonders of the world are overshadowed by
The smile that you wear.

LXXXII

In the realm of human capability, she stands as a beacon of superiority, transcending the limitations often attributed to her gender. She embodies the very essence of existence, possessing an emotional depth and cognitive prowess that eclipses that of her male counterpart. While physical strength may elude her at times, she possesses a unique ability to nurture and sustain life—a testament to her resilience and indomitable spirit.

LXXXIII

Fragile yet fierce, I dare to dream,
Wounded but resilient, in life's tumultuous stream.
I fight for what's right, questioning my worth,
In the depths of my soul, emotions give birth.
Delusions dance, fantasies take flight,
A vessel of passion, burning bright.
In the tapestry of existence, flawed and free,
I am simply me, in all my complexity.

LXXXIV

Life around you doesn't stop, Life goes by its own pace.
It won't stop if you fail, Won't stop if you fall.
It stops for no one.
So, it's better to Learn to pick yourself up,
Correct yourself, Discipline yourself.

LXXXV

She was a sight so beautiful,
That my tired eyes found solace.
Every time my eyes met hers, it's no wonder
The roses are jealous of her.

LXXXVI

When you learn empathy,
You will realize what it actually means:
To not only hear, But experience.

LXXXVII

I count only to lose count.
I feel alive only to feel blue.
I succumb to otherwise,
Like I succumb to you.
I fail to win.
I see to be clear.
I overlook what I get.
I forget that I remember,
I remember only to forget.
I win to fail.

LXXXVIII

Nothing so special about her,
Yet extraordinary she is.
Her impatience is derived from insecurities.
It's very obscene as why
people's acceptance she cares for.
She often forgets what she is, a beautiful woman
who is profound.

LXXXIX

Whatever I expressed to you,
Was never a lie.
It is from the depths of my heart,
but probably an unclear tie.
I failed to make you understand how divine my love is,
And you failed to understand,
telling me you're someone else's.

XC

A girl of deep temperament, her shyness veils her might,
Untangling every loose end, she strives for what's right.
In moments of vulnerability, she shares her heart's
cries,
Obsessing over the unattainable, her longing sighs.
Yet with each passing day, healing draws near,
For time is her ally, and solace will appear.

XCI

This time, right here,
Is all that you've got and all that you have lost.
Take a moment. Fixate to abstain from what hurts you.
Cherish your experiences, rejoice in your tears.
You will find light and see what beholds in those stars
that you stare.

XCII

In the intricate tapestry of life, I stand, delicate yet resolute, Bearing scars of battles fought, wounds that silently refute. Championing righteousness, doubting my own value, Within, emotions stir, birthing a kaleidoscope of hue.
In the realm of imagination, illusions pirouette and spin, Passions ablaze, igniting the soul from within. In this grand narrative, flawed yet authentically me, I exist, a testament to life's beautiful complexity.

XCIII

In the elaborate dance of belief, time becomes a curious
companion.
Each moment a brushstroke on the canvas of faith,
As uncertainty waltzes with conviction, unveiling the
beauty of belief in its own time.

XCIV

Enveloped in a cloak of perpetual sorrow,
I find myself defined by your love, your scorn,
Driven by your malicious deceit.
In a ceaseless quest to flee the spectre of your memory,
I wander until my footsteps are stained with blood.
Though outwardly a man, within me,
A part remains eternally in mourning,
Haunted by the mere mention of your name.

XCV

I fail to comprehend why you confine yourself within the walls erected by the stone-hearted. There exists a vast expanse beyond mere words, where you are deserving of the universe and all its wonders. Your joy should not be shackled by doubts and uncertainties. Break free from this cage and embrace the boundless liberation that awaits you.

XCVI

Often, we find ourselves immersed in the complexities of life, grappling with unanswered questions that sow seeds of doubt. Even when answers emerge, we may hesitate to embrace their positivity if they diverge from our expectations.
Life's path can be arduous indeed. From the moment awareness dawns, we confront unclaimed sorrows, building barriers and withdrawing into isolation. Yet, within every challenge lies the opportunity for growth, urging us to break free from doubt's shackles and uncover the limitless possibilities that await.